THE ROAD CHOSEN

THE ROAD CHOSEN

Poems, Stories and Reflections for Holy Week

Janet Killeen

wild goose publications · www.ionabooks.com

Copyright © Janet Killeen

Published 2022 by
Wild Goose Publications
Suite 9, Fairfield, 1048 Govan Road, Glasgow G51 4XS, Scotland
the publishing division of the Iona Community.
Scottish Charity No. SC003794. Limited Company Reg. No. SC096243.

ISBN 978-1-80432-002-0
Cover image © Pexels from Pixabay

The publishers gratefully acknowledge the support of the Drummond Trust,
3 Pitt Terrace, Stirling FK8 2EY in producing this book.

All rights reserved. Apart from the circumstances described below relating to non-commercial use, no part of this publication may be reproduced in any form or by any means, including photocopying or any information storage or retrieval system, without written permission from the publisher via PLSclear.com.

Non-commercial use:
The material in this book may be used *non-commercially* for worship and group work without written permission from the publisher. If photocopies of small sections are made, please make full acknowledgement of the source, and report usage to the CLA or other copyright organisation.

Janet Killeen has asserted her right in accordance with the Copyright, Designs and Patents Act, 1988, to be identified as the author of this work.

Overseas distribution
Australia: Willow Connection Pty Ltd, 1/13 Kell Mather Drive,
Lennox Head NSW 2478
New Zealand: Pleroma, Higginson Street, Otane 4170, Central Hawkes Bay

Printed by Bell & Bain, Thornliebank, Glasgow

CONTENTS

Introduction   9

Approaching Jericho   11

    Jericho   12
    Reflection   13
    Biblical references   14

    The tree   15
    Reflection   20
    Biblical references   21

The entry into Jerusalem   23

    Parade   24
    Reflection   25
    Biblical references   25

Days of confrontation   27

    The Temple courts   28
    Reflection   29
    Biblical references   29

    Dust   30
    Reflection   35
    Biblical reference   35

Evenings   37

    Sisters   38
    Reflection   39
    Biblical references   40

    The dancing heart   41
    Reflection   41
    Biblical reference   42

Thursday   43

    For the joy that awaited him (I)   44
    Reflection   46
    Biblical references   46

    That night   47
    Reflection   52
    Biblical references   53

Gethsemane   55

    OMG   56
    Reflection   57
    Biblical reference   57

Friday   59

    The tree's song   60
    Reflection   61
    Biblical references   62

    The Red Road   63
    Reflection   69
    Biblical references   69

    After forty years   70
    Reflection   75
    Biblical references   76

Saturday   77

    Piercings   78
    Reflection   79
    Biblical references   80

    Fathoms   81
    Reflection   82
    Biblical reference   82

Sunday   83

    Resurrection   84
    For the joy that awaited him (II)   85
    Reflection   85
    Biblical references   86

Sources and acknowledgements   87

INTRODUCTION

As I prepared this collection of material for Holy Week, I wanted more than anything else to connect imaginatively with the humanity of Jesus. He is the 'kinsman', our kin as well as our God, and he moved among fallible, flawed, perplexed people, much like ourselves. People saw him and wondered, and even his closest companions did not understand what he meant or why he did certain things. I've used a variety of perspectives to try to get close to the events traditionally known as 'Holy Week'. Some of the events are far from holy: treacherous, hostile and increasingly isolating for the Man at their heart. He comes to us in his isolation, in confrontation and rejection, in the sorrow and anguish he experienced, in order that we might never be alone.

There is a poem by Philip Larkin, 'An Arundel Tomb', which I like very much. In it he describes the stone effigies of an armoured knight and his lady and the sudden *'tender shock'* of seeing the knight's hand, ungauntleted, holding his wife's hand. In this material for Holy Week I would love to create moments of 'tender shock' as we see the hand of God reaching out to us in our frailty and need through the humanity and vulnerability of Jesus, Son of Man.

Janet Killeen

APPROACHING JERICHO

JERICHO

No trumpet-triumph now,
No crash of conquest, as walls
Collapse in dust and terror.
No slaughtering entry
Ravaging men, women, child and beast.
> Instead, a crowd, eager, curious
> Jostling to glimpse
> With desperate, secret hopes of
> Recognition: status, longing, need,
> Confused and buzzing, in a confluence
> Of cries and calls.

A history forgotten,
Or if remembered, only as heroic,
Its horror veiled
And, surely, long ago,
The rubble buried, distant, overgrown.

Only the scarlet cord of Rahab
Stretches taut through centuries,
Saving and salvaging
Within the true King's genealogy.
> And so a beggar, besieged by blindness,
> Elbowed in the crush (all
> Greedy for a view of this man Jesus,
> Each one mouthing, 'A prophet. A king. A healer.
> Could he be the long-awaited?')

Takes hold of Rahab's cord
And cries out,
'Have mercy on me, Son of David!'
Refusing to be silenced.
And still cries out,
'Have mercy on us, Son of David!' Cries
From the silenced mouths of every victim
Besieged by poverty, or war, or terror.
Above the restless tumult of our time
The true King hears,
And he will call them to his presence,
Naming each one, a Son of Honour, healed,
Prized and unforgotten.

Reflection

There is a turning point on this most costly of journeys when Jesus *'sets his face resolutely'* to go to Jerusalem. I have thought of Jericho as a 'gateway' for this journey, a moment when the ironies of history surely could not have been forgotten by him as he approached the town, bringing healing to a blind beggar and healing of soul to an outcast. And it is Bartimaeus who, blind as he was, recognises his true identity, the heir of kings, Son of David. It is the question of kingship, but not of this world, that shapes the days that follow, until the declaration 'King of the Jews' is nailed above him on the cross.

- 'The ironies of history': Joshua's dramatic capture of the city, the escape of Rahab (later to appear in the genealogy of David), the ruthless slaughter of the inhabitants. Are we comfortable with concepts of kingship and power being applied to Jesus, Son of Man, or do we need a radical rethink of what his kingship really means?

- As Holy Week unfolds, we find that leadership and authority are a 'hot topic' among the disciples, right up to the last meal they share with Jesus. He presents an utterly different model to them, and to the church. Can we rediscover that reality, and live in it?

The route from Jericho to Jerusalem was a road of banditry and danger, 'The Red Road', so named for its bloody notoriety. In so many ways, the perilous journey, chosen with eyes wide open, has begun.

Biblical references

Bartimaeus' story is told in Luke 18:35–43 and Mark 10:46–52. Joshua's conquest of Jericho and the escape of Rahab is described in Joshua 6. Rahab's place in the genealogy of David, and therefore of Jesus, is found in Matthew 1:5–6

THE TREE

'How did he know my name?' The old man lingered, smiling as an inner world opened behind his eyes, more vivid to him than the present. I have learned to wait for the stories to come slowly, tasted afresh as they are told. Many people begin with what for them is a mystery and their story is a slow unravelling of a thread. My patients, too, begin with what is for them the moment of change, the tipping place where their symptoms began to gather into something which cannot be borne. So I have learned to wait and watch the movement of hands and shoulders and read the script of lines around the mouth and eyes.

This man sat on a bench by the wall, under the shade of a great tree. Beyond him I could see the rough grey-pink hills with their clumps of rock rose, oregano and lavender, and in the far distance a group of sighing pines. A lizard scuttled into a crack in the rock. The old man's head moved at the faint flicker of sound and his hands touched the stick that leaned beside him. As his head turned I saw the milkiness of his eyes and recognised the cataracts of old age. 'You will find him,' they had said, 'by the wall under the tree. We share food and water at midday and bring him back with us at dusk. Clement sits with him for much of the morning.' And I had found him, comfortable in the afternoon sunlight, a short, round man with tufted white hair, a face crinkled with lines that could have been concentration and irritation, but which were instantly redeemed by the play of laughter and kindness in his words and expression. He sat there, listening to the quiet wind, the bird calls, the bleating and bells of far-off goats.

'I have come to hear your story,' I said, bringing out of my bag what I needed to make notes, and sitting alongside. 'They told you I was coming?'

He nodded and smiled. 'You are collecting the stories for a book, they told me. It is long ago, and in a different land. But I can remember.' And then he said it, the key to his memory. 'How did he know my name?'

I waited for him.

'Names.' He shrugged his shoulders. 'They matter, you know, more than parents realise sometimes. My name, even when I was a child, was shortened. Spoken lovingly, a shortened name is affectionate, but in the mouth of contempt it is spat out. That is how it became. I was very short, you see, even when a child. I was small and a little clumsy, and other children did not want to play with a boy who slowed them down. So I learned to hide, and to dodge behind walls and to climb trees out of sight. I could pretend then that I did not need play or company. When I grew older I learned other ways of hiding. Money.' He laughed and spread his hands. 'If you make enough you can hide behind it. I soon realised that it gave me power and other people needed me – to show them generosity, or lend them money in hard times, or let them off a debt. A pleasant feeling, even when you work for the occupying power and collect their taxes. I realised that there was a kind of pleasure in hearing my name spoken with fear. Over twenty years I gathered money, built up hatred, saw a slow retribution being worked out for every moment of bullying, for my father's rejection of me. I knew what I was doing, but there was no way out of the web I had woven for myself. Like a spider. No one comes calling for fear of being devoured.'

A woman from the house brought us water and wine, bread and olives. We broke the bread together and for a while he sat still in the painful memory of that loneliness. He stirred, his eyes turning as if to search my face for understanding, acceptance. 'I know,' I said. 'Doctors have power like that, to bring healing or to predict death.'

'You understand then. The fascination of power and its loneliness. I married and we had three children, two daughters and a son. My wife died soon after my daughters were married. Of loneliness, perhaps, or the shadow of the hatred that neighbours felt for me and for my work. Dear soul, she never knew. I never told her of my growing discontent. My son left home after her death. He asked for money to travel. I have never seen him since, and that is nearly thirty years ago. There was a story, you know, about the son who ran away and returned to his father. But that was not our story.' I poured wine into cups for us both and we drank together.

'I began to leave the town and go to Jerusalem. Searching perhaps, but hiding from those who knew me. Looking for what? I couldn't have given it a name. Something had stirred in me from childhood, the memorised Scriptures, though they brought no comfort. I remembered the words of the prophet Amos. He said, "You have sold the righteous for silver and the needy for a pair of shoes." I hung around the outer courts of the Temple, hopelessly crying out, "God, have mercy on me," realising that I had nothing left of any worth at all. Week after week I would make that journey, rough and dangerous though it was, just to be in a place where I thought maybe God might hear me. One day I heard a different voice, not a priest or scribe, a man who told a story about a Pharisee and a tax collector, and the tax collector spoke my words, "God, have mercy on me." How did he know that? He gave me hope. He said that the man went home accepted by God. He told other stories too, this Teacher, about the Jericho road and the priest and Levite that left the wounded man to his fate. I will tell you that story before you go.'

I watched carefully and recognised the telltale breathlessness and greyness around the mouth and nostrils. 'Do not rush this,' I said to him gently. 'I can stay as long as you need. I am just glad to find you and have this chance to hear you.' He put down his cup, and sat more easily, his hands resting for a while, but soon eloquent with gesture as he spoke.

'It was some weeks after that. The whole town knew that this Teacher was approaching down the road from the old town to the new. There was a great outcry as old blind Bartimaeus begged for his healing and the crowd stopped and saw him healed. I was on the edge, watching, hoping. Not knowing how I could ever get close to this man who had spoken my words, who didn't seem to bring the heaviness of the Law with him to condemn me. I've never seen such a crowd, pressing down the road towards the narrow streets of the town. I tried to push through to see, but there was no space, and then I was recognised by one of the men who owed me money, and he cursed and shoved me away. I moved away from the crowd to the tree – a great sycamore-fig tree by the side of the road which I used to climb as a boy – and climbed it to give me a view over the heads of the crowd. I felt like a child again. You could hear and feel the roar of excitement as the Teacher and his companions approached the town. They came into view, and stopped, stopped right under the tree and he called to me. "Zacchaeus, come down! I've come especially to visit your house." Everything, everyone, was silent as I climbed down. There were mutters of resentment from the crowd as I led him to my house, but they died away. I spoke very carefully, knowing this was the end of my old life. "I'm giving back everything that I've taken wrongly – four times over. I'm giving half my money and goods to the poor." Can you imagine what he said to me? "Salvation and healing have come to your house today. And do you know who you truly are? You are a true son of Abraham. I have come to find and help desperate people like yourself."'

His smile flooded his features, washing away the lines of age and distress. Once again, I waited for him to resume his story in his own time.

'I dealt with the business as soon as possible. I had not realised what it would be like to see a family restored, a widow fed, a beggar lifted back into work and dignity again. I heard the cry of the needy. I had not realised in all my search for money that giving it away was better than keeping it.' He shrugged expressively. 'Soon I went to Jerusalem, and I was there in those amazing days of resurrection and Pentecost, and I helped – they would not have believed it in Jericho! – with the distribution to the poor in those early days of sharing everything. Then I wanted to travel. I think at heart I wanted to search for my son. I brought gifts to the churches and carried letters, visited almost all those small communities of believers. Then I came here and found a new home. I have not found my son, but I have become part of a family. I helped Lydia with her accounts until my eyes failed, and I live here in Clement's house. Do you know Clement's story? He wasn't called Clement when he was the town jailer!' We laughed together. 'Names, you see. They mean everything.'

The sun had begun to slip towards the mountains and as the shadows lengthened a chill breeze began to stir the dust across the courtyard. Overhead the leaves stirred. 'You will tell these Jericho stories? Perhaps my son will read them, or his children, and know the truth.' Then he reached out a hand to me and sought my face with his blind eyes. 'Tell me, Doctor Luke,' he asked. 'It won't be long?'

'No,' I answered, understanding his meaning. I took his hand in my left, and with my right hand reached to feel the stammering pulse in his neck. I listened to his shallow breath. 'No, dear friend, it won't be long.'

'That is good,' he said. 'I will be waiting, here, under this tree, for him to come.' Even in the growing dusk, his face was lit again with memory. 'He will call me by name again, I think. But this time it will be his house that we go to.'

Reflection

This story, of Zacchaeus hiding up a tree and being called down to entertain Jesus, illustrates wonderfully how the Divine – in all its breadth and kindness – touches the Human Comedy. A marvellous interlude in this journey.

- I have sought to give Zacchaeus a context, a background to his life and, more importantly, to his desperate desire to see this man Jesus. I imagined moments of challenge, personal regrets, remembered teachings, a story heard in the Temple, at work in Zacchaeus' life to bring him to this point. Is this true of the way God makes himself known to us, in your experience?

- The Gospel stories (and the Book of Acts) come to us as a linear narrative. We can cross-reference and compare them, but we perhaps forget that in the space of three years, in comparatively small communities, people would have had repeated sightings of Jesus, heard the news and gossiped the latest stories. Like us, their lives were woven together in complex ways. Is it helpful to imagine some of the characters and events of those three intense years interacting so that we can trace possible patterns of development and change?

Biblical references

Amos 2:6–7, Luke 18:9–14, Luke 19:1–10

THE ENTRY INTO JERUSALEM

PARADE

On a dais, the self-proclaimed god
Rivals the scant sunlight,
Glittering breast encrusted with
Honours terrestrial, dominions
Conquered or claimed.
Rank upon rank of high-stepping soldiery
Swivel and snap to acknowledge him.
The dull sheen and weight of missiles
Lumber on vast-wheeled carriers.
Tanks grind by, their turrets turning,
Gun barrels phallic in salute.
And the hypnotised crowd
Sways as one, in adulation.

*

While on a street, not far,
Perhaps almost parallel,
An alley of the old town, now
Deserted by once-captivated crowds,
Silence falls, and the dust stirs
As the wind is blowing
As it will.
A man on a donkey rides
Patiently, gently,
Towards eternity, showing
      It could be otherwise.

Reflection

In the Gospel accounts, this is the hour of triumph, the hour of acclamation – the roar of the crowd, the strewn cloaks and palm leaves, the confident, excited affirmation of the disciples. How could it turn so quickly, in just the space of a week, to the ghastly silence of the streets leading to Golgotha, to the weeping, comfortless women, to the jeers of religious leaders and their manipulated mob? Was it in the hours after the triumphant entry, when Jesus, at the height of his popularity, did not take the city by storm, that Judas turned away? When the power he saw demonstrated – the blind given sight, the dead raised, the crowds fed – was manifested not in conquest but 'otherwise'?

- Thinking about the concepts of power or kingship, how might we explore 'otherwise'?

Biblical references

Christ's entry into Jerusalem is described in all four Gospels: Matthew 21:1–11, Mark 11:1–11, Luke 19:28–44, John 12:12–19.

DAYS OF CONFRONTATION

THE TEMPLE COURTS

The week began with rage, rage
In the outer court, the tables thrust aside,
Coins spinning into dust, animals
Bleating and scampering
Down streets and alleys, scenting
The breath of life.
Pigeons, uncaged, taking to air
In swirls of gladdening flight.
The money changers, traders in sacrifice,
Cowering as whips of words scoured them,
And religious leaders storing up those words
To turn against him. 'My Father's house.'

Yet even then, when heat and light bore down
On him, and he was ringed with crowds,
Eager, curious, grateful,
Waiting for a miracle, and at their centre
Such hostility, ravenous for error,
A blasphemy, a spike on which he could be hung,
Even then, he turned with tenderness
To see the woman slip unnoticed
To toss her livelihood with love
Into the treasury chest.

It was as if the hills around Jerusalem
Drew closer, pressing in
With thunder riffling always at their backs,

Stifling us with heat,
Cramping and caging us,
And at their core, a man locked in conflict,
One after another, questions, questions,
Traps and snares, baited and poisoned
With malice.
We watched, yet not seeing,
Not understanding, how deadly were their words,
How short the days now left to us,
How perilous the path he walked.

Reflection

The description of the widow giving everything to God in her devotion shines out like a candle in the midst of the gathering darkness. It is difficult to identify the signs of hope and life when hostility and perhaps despair or fear are crowding in, yet Jesus highlights her giving, making it count far more than everything else around him in that moment.

- These last two years have not been easy for so many people. How can we find the signs of hope and goodness in these circumstances? Have there been experiences that can be shared as examples?

Biblical references

Luke 19:45–20:26, Luke 21:1–4, Mark 12:41–44

DUST

The spoken words were for her. I heard them, quiet though they were, in the immense stillness of the noon heat. But the words lettered in the dust and brushed away, those words were for me. In all that turmoil, I read them and knew their meaning. Now, I remember down the long years' perspective the sharp details of that day.

The heat strikes down in vertical columns towards midday, bringing work to a halt. Dogs gasp in shadowed corners, donkeys struggle with their loads to reach the shade of trees. The streets and squares empty themselves of all save slaves and beggars. Imagine the palpable blows of the sun, like a great hammer driving piles into the earth, and the silence as the everyday traffic of the town recedes and the heat fills the emptiness with itself. Then hear, distant at first, then lurching and dragging round corners, the hoarse cry of a crowd: triumph and contempt mingled in some way that is, even now as I hear it in my memory, less than human. Frightening. Feral.

There in the outer court, picked out by the white glare of the light with blue-black shadows crouching beneath them, a crowd of men. Robes, phylacteries, tassels swirling with the passionate energy that had brought them together, and in the midst of them, dragged and now thrown onto the paving stones, a young woman. Dishevelled, her robe ripped at the breast, panting, gulping with pain and terror. My wife. They force her to stumble to her feet and she stands, swaying, plucking helplessly at her clothes, before a man sitting in the colonnade. The crowd of men swells, shouting, jeering, gesticulating, then falling silent to wait for his response. And I, walking home from the Temple site, with my stonemason's hammer over my shoulder, meeting them at that angle of the courtyard.

I could smell their potency, a mixture of hate and lust, directed at her and through her to the man who stepped from the bench in the shade of the pillars and bent down to squat on his heels in the dust near to her.

'Caught in the very act!'

The rankness of their sweat and haste caused their garments to stick to their bodies as they stood, leaning forwards, silent now. Their knuckles fused to the rocks they carried. I could not see her face, could not push through the barrier of their purpose. I could only see the man, bent before her, drawing shapes with his finger, writing in the dust. Where was her lover, that young merchant's son? I had known of him but pretended wearily not to know. He was nowhere near: running, no doubt, from the bed as the crowd approached, taking refuge in his father's money to flee the town.

Was it inevitable, this moment of exposure and the months of unfaithfulness that led to it? Even now, years later, I wonder if it could have been different. Who and what we are is hidden deep within the core of us, as it is when you split the rock and find crystal beauty or hidden flaw or strength to sustain the weight of the building. Only that testing, splitting pressure can show us ourselves. I was approaching thirty, a master mason, working on the Jerusalem Temple site. My work was a joy to me, as I believe it is to all craftsmen, and I look back now on the miracle of that gleaming Temple rising into the sky, a glory of light and air created from marble so brilliant that it seemed to magnify the very light of the sun. After my foot was crushed under a block of stone, I could no longer climb the upper scaffolding walkways, but I worked on the carvings of pomegranate and vine and loved what I did. The sharp precision of the chisel exploring the rock, the release of curve and beauty as the flower and leaf and fruit takes shape. You would call me quiet, I think, perhaps retiring, absorbed in what my hands were making.

She was young, too young at fifteen years to be betrothed to a man nearly twice her age. Her father, I remember, eager to marry her off, the young daughter left on his hands when his wife died. There was little love in that home, and she was thrust out into marriage. I could provide for a wife with a good home, a maidservant for her, respect in the village. And I loved her. She was beautiful beyond my describing, but a wild creature, trapped, I realised, when I married her. Obedient, frightened, often hiding from me at first: then her fear became anger, scorn for me in my clumsy attempts to reach her. I had no skill to win or please her. I did not, could not know even how to speak with her. After the accident, she did not hide her contempt: 'I had no choice in marrying you,' she said. 'And now you are lame.' A door closed between us. Perhaps it would have helped if there had been a child in those early years, but I could not wish a child to have been conceived in contempt or reluctance. So it was. I, absorbed in my work; she alone, afraid, desperate. It is no wonder that she was drawn to a young man who gave her excitement, the pleasure of her youth and dreams again. As I have said, I knew, but chose not to know. I saw the looks, heard the whispers, but hoped somehow I might find her again when this had run its course. Never, never would I have brought her to a place of shame. That moment in the Temple court tore across both our lives.

I had been working since dawn: you work in the early hours while the light is pearl and gentle. The blinding white of the marble would burn the eye in the full glare of the day. So, I was returning to the village, crossing the court of the Gentiles at a tangent to leave by the gate to the Kidron Valley. I remember noticing very distinctly in the silence a scuttering lizard on the wall and the arcing swallows high overhead. Then the murmur, eager, almost greedy, which swelled again to demand an answer. I saw the man, bent before her, so that in her shame and terror he was lower than her, creating a small circle of safety around her as he continued to draw their eyes away from her exposed and trembling body to the words he inscribed and then smoothed away repeatedly in the dust between them. The silence again: palpable, quivering in the heat. He rose to his feet to look round at the circle of men, holding their gaze, one by one. 'If you're sure you've never done wrong,' he said, almost carelessly, 'you could throw the first stone.'

Then he bent down again and continued his writing. A strange unease, almost embarrassment, passed like a spasm among the crowd, and then they moved away, each remembering some other purpose. When they had gone, he stood up again, drawing her eyes and lifting her head with his gaze – eye to eye, as no other man would look at a woman unless related to her. 'So where are they,' he asked her, gently, 'those who would have condemned you?' I saw her draw together all the frail and shattered pieces of her bid for freedom, wings smashed against the bars of her life – a loveless childhood and marriage, the humiliation of her exposure, her powerlessness as a woman. All of that degradation was held, absorbed, cancelled in the exchange of look for look that passed between them.

'They are not here, Sir,' she answered. I do not know whether she knew that I was present or not.

'Then you, too, are free to go. And you can walk free of past shame.'

Suddenly released, I moved forward from my rigid place in the shadows, my outer cloak ready in my hand to cover her from the stares of strangers as we returned home. She turned to see me, and, as though for the first time, we saw each other clearly, as I walked towards her. And I glimpsed again the words in the dust, before the man bent and finally brushed them away. 'Go, love … again.' Words from the prophet Hosea.

I have often wondered how it was that the finger of God wrote upon the stone tablets of Moses. Were the words incised with fire, chiselled out of living rock? Or what of the fingers that wrote upon the wall of Belshazzar? I saw the finger of God here, lean, brown, a workman's hand much like my own, and it spelled out healing, not judgement.

And so we left Jerusalem and its neighbourhood. There is always work for a mason, even with a crippled foot, and we travelled first to Caesarea Philippi, where I found work on the summer palace. Soon, we moved to Corinth, seeking a new beginning and a new community, and gradually love, trust, kindness grew between us. Shame fled away, and our children were born. And our firstborn, our daughter, your mother, we called Keziah, after Job's daughter, that she would always have an equal inheritance with her brothers.

It is now many years since my dear wife died. All our years of healing and happiness have long outweighed those early griefs, but I want you, my dear granddaughter, to understand and remember our story. Make sure that it is told, so that others understand how she was treated on that day, and how he raised her up to dignity and hope. It is forty years ago, and now Jerusalem itself has fallen into ruin. Those magnificent walls besieged, and the stone blocks, so crisply carved and joined that you could not pass a feather between them, all crashed into rubble, split, wrecked. A desolation.

But what was written in the dust remains.

Reflection

The beautiful story of the woman 'taken in adultery' found in John's Gospel is something of a mystery. Wonderfully characteristic of Jesus' response to women and to those labelled 'sinners', does it belong to material gathered by Luke and transferred to John during the first centuries of transcription? We will probably never know. However, the mounting tension and challenge of the story, the confrontation in the Temple courts, the bitter hypocrisy and its exposure by the wit and compassion of Jesus, could well belong to the final week of conflict that we call Holy Week. So I have placed it here, where its themes of mercy, human dignity restored, and the tender loving-kindness of God shine out in contrast with the judgemental attitudes of religious legalism.

- Has anything surprised or challenged you as you have read this imagined account of the story that is traditionally known as 'the woman taken in adultery'?

Biblical reference

John 8:2–12

EVENINGS

SISTERS

Always a little different,
Viewed askew in the village.
One, married as her childhood fled
And early widowed,
Now returned to keep her brother's house
(That dreamer among olive groves). And her sister,
Fey, an isolate, who knows her thoughts, or history?
Don't ask. Single, all of them now,
A strange household. Not like us.
Why does he go to them
Finding a home there, time after time?
Surely he knows the village
Whispers? Why speak with them
As if with equals, bringing them visions
Of life and love, teaching them, as if, mere women,
They could possibly understand?
What welcome could they offer?

*

Food and rest; the normal stress
Of domestic busyness; small and unresolved
Frustrations, shared and easily forgiven;
Uncomplicated, everyday love;
The quietness of attentive listening.
Calm, after each day's snarling disputes,
And to and fro of endless, sharp controversy.

The generosity of a home,
To one who came and found
No other home was opened to him.
A homely, ordinary kindness, an imperfect family,
Offering unhesitating welcome.

Reflection

Martha and Mary and their brother Lazarus: a home which, we're told, Martha *'opened'* to him, and which seems to have been a place of refuge in the brief time left, the evenings away from the city. Who were they? We know so little, even though there is speculation that Mary of Bethany was Mary Magdalene. We never hear a word from Lazarus. We know of the momentous event of Lazarus' death and his *'coming forth'* alive from the tomb in response to the loud cry of Jesus; we know that Jesus, sharing the anguish of the sisters and his insight into human mortality and loss, *'wept'*. At the heart of that event, we have the profound conversation between Jesus and Martha leading to that momentous statement: *'I am the resurrection and the life.'*

But all too easily remembered about Mary and Martha and quoted is the momentary frustration of one sister with another, *'Don't you care that I'm overworked here. Tell her to give me a hand.'* It is so easy to condemn Martha for her lack of 'spirituality', when maybe she knew she was loved enough to be real. I've given Martha a possible past – a girl early married and soon after widowed, returning to her brother's home to run his household. The extraordinary thing is that each of these individuals is unmarried. There were widows (sadly, many of them, judging by the provision that had to be made for them in the Early Church), but an unmarried single woman was unusual in those days, and in that culture. It is likely that the sisters would have been looked at askance, yet their Bethany home is a place where Jesus feels relaxed, safe, familiar and trusted enough to be brought into a family disagreement. What he says to Martha about Mary, and for everyone to hear, is that she has made a choice. He had made his choices long before knowing both their freedom and their cost. So what he affirms, remarkably, is her right to choose; her right to listen and learn.

- Yet how many situations are there in the world, two thousand years later, where women *still* have no right to choose, and no right to learn. Why has it taken so long for the church to wake up to this?

In his relationship with Mary and with Martha, he shows a deep knowledge of and respect for their individuality. The things that were carried secretly, perhaps with pain and longing, in their hearts (and ours), are the things known to him and honoured. To be celebrated, if not now, through all eternity.

Biblical references

John 11:1–44 (especially verses 17–36), John 12:1–3, Luke 10:38–42

THE DANCING HEART

Who sees the dancing heart?
None save one
Whose steady gaze
Penetrates the cage of bone.

Who hears the singing veins?
One who alone
Is unafraid
Of the heart's bright flood.

Who grasps the hidden bone,
Testing its strength?
One who will hold the enduring frame
Beyond the dust.

Reflection

There are stories in the Gospels that show with great clarity Jesus' insight into the hidden longings and sorrows of the human heart. The stories told about Mary and Martha illustrate this powerfully, as does the encounter with Zacchaeus. Another account of such a meeting is the conversation with the Samaritan woman in John (4:2–42). It can be an exciting and liberating way to explore familiar stories if we ask ourselves, 'What does Jesus recognise about this person that society is not seeing, or is misjudging?'

- This poem works like a riddle, a series of questions. Do you find its questions challenging or meaningful?

Biblical reference

Psalm 139:1–18

THURSDAY

FOR THE JOY THAT AWAITED HIM

I

Once, before time, before any need of form
Or measurement, or name
(All being known in joyous love and oneness),
Dwelling in darkness, richer than the core of the sun,
More dazzling with radiance, brilliant
With passionate mysteries dreamt in the mind of God.
Life, brimming with abundance, far beyond
The unknown, waiting depths
Of seas or forests, still uncreated and unnamed.
A ceaseless celebration,
An endless delight of inexpressible glory,
A jubilation of angels.

Then (and who knows when?) the choice, the risk:
To make known, reveal, a form, a Being
Comprehensible to faith, with all its possibility
Of love and reciprocity.
And all its possibility of loss.

A Word spoken: a Word that upholds
Universes, dimensions of space,
Pathways of stars exceeding all imagination.
Then, the naming of an unfolding creation,
Calling it into form and presence:
Time, space, substance, light.

Dark. Day. Stars, sun, moon, night.
Fern and tree, grass, flower, fruit.
And creatures of gait and flight and fluid motion.
Then, Man and Woman.

*

And all things subject now to time,
In the eternal watchfulness of the sustaining Word,
To choose again: to lay aside that form of God
(Ignored, rejected or at the best, faintly perceived and barely understood)
And enter through the confining womb,
And narrow gate of birth, to show in human form
Through thirty years,
The true and loving, patient nature of Himself.

And in the last acts of love,
To hold and wash with tender carefulness
The hardened, grimed and weary feet of friends
(His own unwashed),
And tear the bread and offer wine
For their refreshment.
And hear, so soon, how their feet fled from him,
As his captors trampled the quiet garden.
Then (he who is Word and Life) kept
Silent in the face of lies,
And the unrelieved torment of sun-darkening death.

Reflection

I began writing this poem with a passage from the letter to the Philippians in mind. Paul captures amazingly, in very few words, the drama of Christ's choice of servanthood and his exaltation to glory. It echoes very powerfully the story of the washing of the disciples' feet described in John. As I wrote the poem there was so much to try to put into words and imagination falters! However, I found the image of the feet becoming more and more significant – feet that are washed and refreshed … yet no one offers to wash the feet of Jesus. Feet that approach with ominous tread. Feet that run away.

- Do you find it helpful to enter imaginatively into a scene that is described in the Gospels? And if so, might it be useful to focus on one particular image or on one set of sensory impressions? Have you experienced fresh insight into a biblical narrative by taking a totally different viewpoint – a bystander, an outsider, even someone hostile to what is going on?

Biblical references

Philippians 2:6–11, John 13

THAT NIGHT

Silent feet, silent tongue. That is how they train you. And we don't tell them: sharpened ears, sharpened sight. We see and hear everything. When we can snatch the odd time off, between dinner and bed, maybe, or in the heat of the afternoon when the mistress is resting, we meet up in the marketplace, or the wine shops down the alley by the Gate and catch up on the gossip. We all know one another, share the same secret life. Comradeship. Where the mask can slip a little. Small jokes. Kindness. Maybe even the hope of a future husband or a wife, if the small savings can be garnered away and the luck turns. Who knows?

But this evening. How can I begin to talk of it? It's very late now, but there are still lights in many houses, and torches carried along the streets, and the crunch of soldiers' feet, the scuff and scurry of sandals, and a distant murmur of unrest, like the growl in the back of a wild dog's throat. The wild dogs that hang around the rubbish, snarling.

Sharpened ears, sharpened sight.

I'm trying to sort it in my head. Who I was, even yesterday, is not who I feel I am today. It began, I think, with that odd moment by the well. I'd drawn up the water, filled the great jar, and was hoisting it up to carry it through the streets, the last of many, but this one to be carried upstairs to the guest room.

I was tired. Maybe I've always been tired, since the day my father sold me in payment of his debts. Just out of childhood, twelve years old, and I remember my mother weeping. Down in the dust, begging him. And he shook her off and sent me north to the city with a friend of his, in a cart full of new wineskins, and goatskin rugs, stinking and hot, and I sat still as stone and the tears have never come. You could say I was lucky. When I hear other stories, I know that's true in a way. I came to the house of a good woman and her family, none of them cruel or rough, and she put me in the care of the steward and the cook to train me to serve at table, and to learn to prepare the food. They were kind, mostly, except when the household got very busy at the festivals; and once a year I was given a gift of money, and clothing, and the hope grew that, one day, they might set me free. Although, when you think about it, freedom is a blade with two edges, and one points towards you. There's no life in those dark and churning streets for a woman on her own.

Ten years since I came, just a child, and now I carry the water and attend to the guests, and serve at table, silent, watchful. Just a pair of hands, really, until those odd hours of fleeting laughter and talk in the stolen moments of the day or night.

So, I'd filled the great pitcher, and turned, feeling the balance of it, straightening up to begin the walk to the house, and a man stopped me. 'Daughter,' he said. 'Let me carry that for you.' I thought he was joking, or if not, maybe it was one of the slaves like myself, wanting to give me a hand. But men don't carry the water. That's a woman's job.

'No,' I said, slowly facing him, unsure how to deal with this. If it was a joke, it was a bad one. If it was a genuine offer of help, I needed to be sure that I could trust this man, and know he was not looking for any favours. I looked: I had never seen him before, and even though I looked hard at him, I could not tell you the details of his face.

'My daughter,' he said again. 'You are very tired. Let me take this for you.' As I looked at him, I felt as if he knew me, and I was afraid that the crying might begin and never stop. 'Don't worry,' he said, very gently, and took the heavy jar, and balanced it carefully, and walked away. A few heads turned as he walked up the street, and a couple of men began to follow him. Gathering myself as soon as I could, I followed too, anxious and hot as the sun was now moving further overhead. But I need not have worried. He took the pitcher to the house, climbed the outside steps to the upper room, while the two men behind him went inside to talk to the master. They had taken no notice of the man. As I came near to the door, he came downstairs, smiled, and was gone. I went to the back of the house, puzzled, silent. Then the master of the house came in almost immediately and gave directions for the upper room to be prepared for thirteen guests to eat the Passover meal.

There was then no time to waste. Food to prepare, not just for the family, but for these guests. The room to be spotless and the furniture and cushions ready for them to recline around the long table. Lamps to be set out and wicks trimmed. The pitcher of water, the jug, bowl and towels for their feet to be washed. My job, before the meal could be served. You could tell, from the whispered excitement in the house, that these were important guests, and everything must be perfect. The silent, sharp-eyed service that I was trained for.

The sun turned red and sank lazily beneath the clouds that rise from the Great Sea, far west – and I have never seen it, but so they tell me. Dusk gathered in corners and spread slowly over the city and the lamps were lighted, and torches flared in the streets. I remember standing at the doorway, out of sight, as the men came up the stairs, bringing with them the sweat and restlessness of the day and its dust in their hair and clothing, and on their feet and sandals. I stood ready with the bowl and jug and towels, waiting for them to take their ease on the cushions around the low table. They were excited, talking and gesturing as they took their places and I noticed, as you do, the way in which they pushed for position to lie near the head of the table.

They did not notice as I moved forward, expecting to kneel and begin the task of easing their feet and cleansing them for the meal ahead. Nor did they notice as he came in, and as he silently took the bowl and jug and towel from me, and began my work, the slave's work. Finger on lips to me, and that same steady look, the gentle smile, then the intense focus on the feet of his friends, washing them with great gentleness, as if caressing them with kindness. At first they thought it was the slave: so familiar was the pattern of hospitality, they barely recognised that it was happening. Then one of them, a burly man, who seemed by the strength of his voice and presence to have some sort of leadership, swung round and realised. He was loud in his protests, loud with the strong accent of the north, but his friend, who I see now was the true leader of the group, persisted. He was red-faced with embarrassment as he submitted, and the rest of the group were frozen, I thought, speechless, as their leader washed their feet and dried them, carefully. Tenderly. It takes a long time to wash twelve pairs of feet. The room waited, the meal forgotten, and the evening gathered itself around the table. I felt the darkness waiting as if about to spring. The oil lamps held it at bay.

Then at last the figures came to life. The meal began and I ran to and fro with the platters of meat and bread, the wineskins to pour into the jugs and then to cups – and it takes a steady hand – and all the special ceremonial food of the Passover. I watched them, and listened as the conversation rose, with argument and flourishes of hands and arms and food and cups spilt onto the table. 'Who's the most important?' they were saying. 'Which of us will be in the place of power when the Kingdom comes?'

'Well,' I thought to myself. 'Have you learned *nothing*?' But I had to go then and get more food and more to drink. When I returned, the group had quietened. 'Is it me, is it me?' they were asking, but I do not know the question.

There was one moment as I lingered when he stood and took the bread and broke it, tore it apart, and said a strange thing. 'My body,' he said and handed it to them.

When I went back, to clear the table, one of them was rising to his feet, and leaving hurriedly, and the stir of air at his passing caused all the lamps to splutter and the darkness entered as he left. I brought light quickly and renewed the lamps, but the mood had changed. They shifted uncomfortably, then stood together to sing the psalm and left down the steps and into the dark streets.

I did not get away until much later that night, after the first cockcrow, but you could sense that rising murmur of excitement, anger, fear, call it what you like, it was all those things, and the city still hums with it. I joined old friends at the wine shop and heard the stories that were running round like jackals about a betrayal and arrest in a garden. Malchus, slave of the High Priest, came in clutching his ear, and we all marvelled at his story, and touched his ear, and the tale grew of the man in the garden and the followers who ran away. Anna came bursting in with the thrill of her story, always a gossip. 'I recognised him, I tell you,' she said, hands on hips. 'He was one of them, one of those men from Galilee. You could tell it by his voice. And I've seen him around with that Jesus. Big fellow, but not so big now, I can tell you. Three times he said he didn't know him.' Others came with the details of the show trial at the High Priest's and then Herod's court, and we knew the next step would be the Romans. The taste of the story turned bitter to all of us, and we found ourselves scattering, even the most talkative frightened by the events that were overtaking us, events of great heaviness, terrible things. I thought of the man. He had called me, 'Daughter'. No one had done that since the day I left my home, a slave.

Two of my friends were walking up ahead as I returned through the alleys to the house. Fragments of their talk reached me, and they stay with me now. 'They say he sold him for thirty pieces of silver,' they were saying. The slave price. The price my father got for me.

Reflection

Some commentators have suggested that the mysterious man carrying the water from the well was Jesus himself. His disciples just did not recognise him – just as they were unable to imagine that he would be a menial servant for their sakes. No man would carry the water from the well. It was a woman's job. And it was the most menial of jobs to wash feet. Here we have an extraordinary story in which Jesus 'turns the world upside down' – as he did throughout his entire ministry. To the slave girl, looking on, there are so many mysteries. The total incomprehension of the friends as they continue to argue about who will have a position of power in the coming Kingdom. The words spoken as the bread is broken. The sudden departure of one of the group. We have the advantage (or disadvantage) of hindsight, but they were people watching events unfold for the first time, and some elements of that last extraordinary meal would have shocked, even horrified, them: the reference to blood, and the statement that one of the disciples would betray their Master. 'Is it me, is it me?' is their uncertain response.

- Imagine that you, like the slave girl, are watching these events. Try to put aside what you know and the way it has been interpreted. What most strikes you and how – with bewilderment, horror, sympathy? Is hindsight an advantage or disadvantage when we come to the biblical narrative?

- And then there is the extraordinary, symbolic act of washing the feet of the disciples. The lesson so hard to learn, that the leader is, first of all, the servant. Is the symbolism of washing feet (so often part of Maundy Thursday's liturgy) still powerful and effective today or do we need to look afresh at what servanthood and humility look like, both in society and in the church?

Biblical references

John 13, Luke 22:7–13

GETHSEMANE

OMG

Oh my god! A whooping cadence of delight,
Teetering arm-in-arm out of the club
On parapets of three-inch heels.
Clutching each other,
Shrieking gleeful frost-breath
Into a cold night.
An amber smothering of streetlight
Hides the stars.

Oh my god! Uncomplicated joy of life
Expressed. Not prayer or praise,
Or formal collect,
But collected nonetheless,
And heard and held in keeping
Until a time, years hence,
When weeping, one will say,
Thank God for that, at
The safe return of a child.
And the other cry out,
God, where the hell are you?
In the slow-turning hours
Of chemo treatment,
Waiting alone for results.

Reflection

No one can easily imagine the anguish of those hours in the Garden, nor the pain of that shamed, resentful identification, the moment when all choices fuse together into the act of love and obedience that reaches its climax on the cross. The Gospel narrative shows us that no one could accompany Jesus in those hours of struggle: his friends fell asleep only a few yards away from him. Instead, we can see how Jesus accompanies us, endures and identifies with the suffering of the world he came to heal. In the poem, I've taken the all too frequent exclamation 'Oh my God', and turned it from 'meaninglessness' to prayer.

- How do you react to this idea?
- What for you is the most significant aspect of the struggle described in the Garden of Gethsemane?
- What *is* prayer?

Biblical reference

Mark 14:32–50

(I've chosen Mark's account of the Garden of Gethsemane because, traditionally, he drew on Peter's account of Jesus' ministry. The account seems to burn with the regretful, vivid remembrance of those hours and the night that followed.)

FRIDAY

THE TREE'S SONG

Along hushed streets,
The crowd aghast, the stones silent,
Yet the wood grain sang to him.
> (The weight of government crushed across
> His shoulder, rough and splintering,
> Jarring against the thorns.)

The wood sang to him:

'You saw the seed fall into darkness
From the tree's height,
A fall, alone, a dying.
Until the earth split as
Leaves unfurled in tenderness:
A stem, a sapling, thrusting skywards
Through thirty years of growth.

'You know the touch of wood
Planed and caressed to light,
Grain enlivened, smoothed and ready,
Not this, rough and ribbed,
Cut down in haste
And sawn for bloody purpose.'

> (Still the grain sang to him
> Each step accompanied
> By the deep silent thrumming of the wood.)

'And after, thrown down
And shamed, we will be fuel
Taken by stealth tonight for some poor man's fire,
Our breath given for warmth,
For light and comfort.
So, another song.

'As you too will be cut down,
And all your dreamers will see only death.

'But you will rise:
As timber to uphold the sky,
Light breaking in brilliant leaf,
A flame to burn
In unimaginable
Hearths and hearts.'

Reflection

The journey through the streets of Jerusalem, the Via Dolorosa, is most wonderfully imagined in the ancient Stations of the Cross. I knew that I could add nothing, no new perspective, to that tradition. Instead, the phrase came to me, *'Still the tree sang to him'*, and this poem began to emerge. I imagined Christ the carpenter and the feel of the wood against his neck and shoulder.

One of the joys of working with wood is to see the grain emerge like silk as it is planed smooth and then waxed. It must have given him delight in his years of apprenticeship and then as a craftsman. But this wood has been brutalised. How might that have felt?

I imagined the sounds of that journey. The raucous shouts of hatred that would still linger in the ears, the clipped commands of the military escort, the excited yet fearful buzz of the crowd dying away to shocked silence, the weeping of women. And so the tree sings to him, responding to its Creator, accompanying him when all other friends have drawn away.

- When we allow ourselves to imagine, can it lead us into deeper truth?

- Trees figure significantly in the overarching narrative from Eden to Revelation. John Donne wrote: *'We think that Paradise and Calvary, Christ's cross, and Adam's tree, stood in one place'* (from 'Hymn to God, my God, in my sickness'). And towards the very end of the Book of Revelation there is a vision of the river of the water of life and the tree along its banks: *'And the leaves of the tree are for the healing of the nations.'* Do any of these images hold special meaning for you?

Biblical references

Luke 23:1–37, Revelation 22:1–2

THE RED ROAD

All those years ago. No, I've never forgotten. Could never forget. But it is a story hidden away. Kept secret. They helped me at first, a woman watching with them through all those desperate hours, who went away weeping, shrouding her head, and then joining them in the first glad, crazy days of news and celebration. There were soon crowds of us. Crowds that I hid among, watching how the wind would turn, where the luck might fall for me. Always on the outside, watching, until who I was could be forgotten. Then like so many of them, I fled away to a new life, a new city, and began again, and now you find me, after so many years. Now you come and stir those memories again, sharp as the edge of a knife. But it is right to tell you my story. It all comes together now and must not be forgotten.

Always crowds, and always at the fringe. I can see it now, feel it even, in these hands that were once as light as butterflies. You'd never know, looking at them now, lumpen and twisted with age. Working the crowd. That's what we did. You could feel the tension in the hairs on the back of your neck – like eyes, I said they were, sensitive to every move and shift of what was going on. He would be at the edge, waiting to run on soles as soft as a cat, and I would take the purse, and gut it, catching the coins unclinking in my hand and getting them to him. Sometimes a bracelet, slit from a wrist, or a necklace. I was his woman. Yes, I know the names many called me. He never did.

We never knew any other kind of life. An alley in a back street, a rough childhood learning to dodge the blows: beg, scrounge, steal. If I hadn't met him, it would have been the streets for me, and the brutal handlings of a garrison town. But I met him, and we made a life, not love as you'd call it, but tender in its way and kind even, and a sort of home, a stinking rat hole in a back street, but the only place we knew where we could hide, and find enough love to survive and share what we could after the fence had taken his cut. We scraped by ... How old was I? I don't know. I don't remember much of my childhood. A woman who sang, sometimes, and drank other times, and shoved me out of sight behind a curtain when the soldiers came to her. As soon as I could stagger about I begged for her and scavenged the rubbish in the Valley. I met him there, my Dismas, beggar like myself, but already sharp-eyed and quick to slide alongside a rich man and feel for the fat purse and slip his hand between the buckles. So, I left my mother; left her, I remember with her head in a shawl, crooning, and the jug swinging empty from her hand. The pity of it, I know now.

We scraped by, I said. Just enough, and sometimes that bit extra for a drink and a hot meal at a tavern and a laugh and song with mates. That was how we learned about him. The crowds that gathered round him, and weaving through the crowd, people like us, begging or stealing or both as the people hung on his words. Sometimes they'd listen to him and come away generous with goodwill, and others, angry and proud, because he'd stirred them up, made them look at themselves and their religion. We had no time for religion, me and Dismas, it was only for the already good and the wealthy. If you were rich, God had blessed you. If you were poor, begging and thieving, scavenging on the rubbish, then somehow God must have no time for you. That's what we thought.

That's why, when I first caught the sound of his voice, it brought me up short. The ground was thick with people, from all over. You had the rough accents of the north, and the western voices from the coast around Tyre and Sidon as well as the city voices, sharp as splinters, and the rich had to rub shoulders with the poor, with the farm workers and shepherds and women of the streets, and us. You could see them twitch themselves away, but it's hard to do so in a crowd and everyone pressing forward to hear him. So, just for a moment, I listened too and forgot to grope for purses and bags and trinkets. And he said, right out, 'Blessed are the poor … The hungry … the weeping ones … the ones who feel excluded. And woe to you rich … and well-fed.' I can still remember it. It turned the world upside down for me, although of course we laughed about it that night, counting out what we'd stolen. What would he know about poverty and hunger? But what if it were true? Well, that began it, I suppose, for both of us, though I never realised it until much later.

We followed him, we had to, the pickings were too good, but with never the same ease of mind, like something uncomfortable pricking you, like a thorn in the palm of your hand.

We were there in the crowd, me with my light fingers feeling the purses of the rich, the offerings of the righteous, and slitting them open silently, and my man at the edge waiting to vanish with the pickings. We were there, and he saw us. I know that. Even as he began the story, his eyes moved around the crowd and saw us; and he told the story of the man on the road to Jericho, who fell among thieves, and the outsider who rescued him. He saw us, and knew us, and neither of us could quite forget it. Not fear. He wasn't going to denounce us. No, the kind of knowing that can get inside you, like water in a crack in a rock, and one day it will split you open. We knew the Jericho road: rich pickings if you were careful, but violence too, and some of it brutal. My man had done that, he and his partner, beaten up travellers and left them for dead. The Red Road, the Bloody Road, we called it. If you travelled alone or at night, you were a fool.

Months later, it was, and all the city humming with the preparation for the Festival, and the rumours that folk like us could hear because our ears were always to the crack in the door, undercurrents of suspicion and hate and fear. The plans that were at work to trap and catch him, destroy him, that travelling preacher who dared to say that the poor were blessed, and who turned out the money changers in the Temple courts. All the city murmuring and throbbing and pilgrims travelling in from everywhere.

My man came back to me after two days away, tunic brown with blood. And blood that had gathered in the fine creases of his hands, sticky even then after hours hiding in the caves in the hills. So, when he came home to me with his bloodied hands and hopeless eyes, I knew something had changed for him. Even now, I remember what he said and how his eyes fixed on me. 'I killed him. Slit his throat, the blood spouting out like a goat at a festival. No, not that little runt of a fellow in Jericho. The fat traitor that works in Bethany. He struggled. Called out when he felt the prick of the knife under his ear. So, I killed him. It's not the first. But this one. This one sticks to me.' I brought water for him and washed his stained hands and took his tunic away to burn it, but we heard them clashing down the street, turning into the alley, jeering as they came. 'Come out, rat, we know who you are, where you hide. You were seen.' Even now, I remember the intake of breath, the horror and terror of the moment. We knew the punishment for theft and murder, especially the murder of a tax collector. The Roman law, in all its force, crashed in on us.

Two witnesses, a moment's trial, a flogging. They were eager to get the execution out of the way before the day of the Feast. They hauled him up. And alongside was his partner, angry and cursing that he had been caught, and that other man, that unforgettable preacher. What had he ever done to suffer this? I stayed with him, with the other women, and some of them I know now, and they helped me to survive afterwards.

We all heard the words spoken through that terrible day: the heat and then the darkness. The mockery, the courage, the long-drawn-out writhing pain of it. How do men think of these terrible things to do to one another? I heard his partner cursing, full of rage and fear and pain.

'Why don't you save us?' he sneered. 'You're supposed to be the Messiah. Well, prove it!'

And I heard my Dismas answer him, 'Don't you have any respect for God? We're getting what we deserve for our crimes. But this man has done nothing wrong.' I watched him turn, twisting on those terrible nails and heaving himself forward to see this man, Jesus, and speak directly to him. 'Jesus,' he gasped. 'Jesus, remember me when you come into your kingdom.'

I saw them gaze at one another, two men utterly unlike each other yet now sharing an understanding so deep they could have been brothers. To speak, to turn and look, to hold that gaze was agony, unbearable, yet they did so.

'I tell you the truth,' Jesus said to him, 'you and I will be together in paradise today.'

It was enough to hold him through the torture of the rest of those hours and the brutal mercy of the breaking of his legs so that he slumped forward and could no longer breathe. And I thought of him, with his friend, walking in the garden of paradise whilst we women washed the tormented bodies and prepared them for burial – I would not let them sling him into the Valley until I had washed and kissed his eyes and hands.

I have often thought of the story of the man attacked by bandits that Jesus told. And I realise that he was like them. Strung up like them, like a thief; and he was the one who fell among thieves, the victim, bloody and battered and his life stolen away; and he was the man riding to rescue us, the outsider, the one who got off his donkey to bind and bandage, pour in the stinging wine, the soothing oil. And I remember too, and it carried me through the days and weeks and months that followed, that he said, 'Blessed are those who weep. One day you will laugh again.'

That is my story, Dr Luke. You've found me here and heard me and you can see how my story and my man's story weave in and out of those years when Jesus taught the people about mercy and justice, and then showed us exactly what he meant.

And afterwards? After that terrible day? I was taken in by one of the women, given a home. We were all sisters. They taught me how to sew and bake and I travelled with one of them as her maid and care for her now. She is very old, but her memory is still sharp, even of those days more than sixty years ago, when she was a young girl. Wonderful stories. I know you have come all this way to see her: let me go and see if she is strong enough to join you in the garden. I will bring drinks for you, and then leave you. These stories are precious to us women. Secret. But now it is time for them to be told.

Reflection

The Gospel stories sometimes stand in isolation, although, in reality, the events and people described must have woven in and out of each other. People would have travelled, gossiped, wondered, shared. That is what I imagined might have happened in the story of the man traditionally called Dismas and why I connected him with the story of the 'Good Samaritan' and the earlier, revolutionary teaching of what are called 'The Beatitudes'. Something about Jesus in those hours of suffering, perhaps his steadfast demeanour and words of forgiveness, or things that Dismas had heard before and pondered, led him to turn away from cursing and raving in agony to his simple request which is so wonderfully answered.

- This 'Road Chosen' has brought Jesus to the cross. Do you think it is a coincidence that these two thieves accompany him, or is this, too, 'chosen'? If so, what meaning do you feel lies at the heart of this episode?

Biblical references

Luke 23:32–43, Luke 10:29–37, Luke 6:17–26

AFTER FORTY YEARS

So, I have returned. The end and the beginning join here, now. That raw recruit, blistered from training camp and the forced march from the port. And the veteran, due to take a pension and settle – where? I do not know. So many years lie between those two soldiers, so long a time, so great a distance, that I can hardly recognise them both as myself. Only the place remains.

Memory jolts backward to see him then, to smell his sweat, to feel his queasiness after the voyage, his ears jarred with sounds. The stamp of booted feet; the slap of hand to weapon; the raucous chants of song and curse as the company moves up through the winding streets away from the docks; the rasping rise and fall of his breath. His fears of stumbling out of rhythm in the drill, or facing exposure for brass unpolished, leather dulled. The thousand insecurities of a posting abroad. Untried. Unskilled. Eighteen years old.

Since then, years of soldiering and peacekeeping in dusty corners of the world, where languages fall strangely on the ear, formed of breath, or liquid like water, not like my familiar harsh consonants of tongue and teeth. Decades spent stamping down uprisings, policing riots, building roads and bridges. The routines of barrack life, the boredom, the easy comradeship of shared drinking; the terrible loneliness of danger. Miles tramped on rough and broken roads. I struggled then: now I can march twenty miles in the day and think nothing of it. A lifetime.

The road swings up through the same hills. And I find that their shapes are scraped on the back of my eyes like no other, and the smouldering scent of a sun-burnt land and the crushed fragrances of herb sting in my nostrils again. A long march, and time to remember as the afternoon sun stretches our shadows beside us. That boy, hungry for manhood, paces beside me, refusing to remember his mother's tears of farewell and his father's indifferent shrug. In all the years since, he never knew when she died, or if she got the one greasy letter sent in those first days of embarkation. His pack weighs heavy, burdened with gear and weapons on thin shoulders, and with the secret load of fear. Mine, too, is heavy, though the familiar weight is easy, but the scent and sight of this place stirs too much that I have chosen to forget, and it clamps down on me, tightening its straps around my chest and heart.

Those early days are a rush and blur of duties and commands for all recruits, but especially in a strange city, a strange country, they overwhelm you. The people lower their eyes so that you cannot see the hostility in their flickering glances. Their talk is pitched in tones and sounds you do not recognise, and the streets are full of strident cries and jostling crowds. You learn to shove and curse through them and feel brutality rise in you to mask whatever may be vulnerable in yourself. A uniform, a blow, a shout, do not need an interpreter to clear the way, and so you learn quickly. Within a few days the army breaks you in, hardens you, so that you can be sent on any duty without disgracing yourself or your unit with weakness. They choose a tough assignment and send along a couple of raw youngsters with a squad of old hands to learn the realities of soldiering.

For me, two weeks into my first posting, it was the guard duty at an execution. Brutal, public warnings of the punishment meted out for crime or insurrection. The stench of blood under a ruthless blazing sky, the cries torn out of men who writhed with the slowness of their dying. A jeering crowd. Silent, anguished women. I remember how I turned to vomit behind a thorn bush, sickened with the horror of it, desperate to escape the scorn of my comrades. And as I turned back, wiping my sour mouth, I saw the man's eyes. Watching me with an expression I could not read, could not understand. Kindness? Pity? Calmness in his eyes, despite the rictus of pain twisting his face.

A day of unendurable length, ending in darkness and the broken indignities of slung bodies and burials, and a guard duty over. My shoulders slapped with rough sympathy by an older soldier, and I stumbled away to seek my manhood among the girls that hung around the bars. I chose one, in the flickering light, because it seemed to me that she still knew how to smile with her eyes not just her mouth, even though she called me 'soldier boy' and pulled me down to her with practised arms and hands that stripped off belt and webbing with accustomed skill. I took her then, and sought her for days and nights afterwards like a draught of forgetfulness, night after night in the dark passageways, and against stones still hot from the day's sun; gritty, sweating, urgent. Until one day she told me. Perhaps it was mine. I would have killed any other man who touched her. Stupid with drink and longing, homesick fool, I said, 'Then marry me.' We had some mumbling civil ceremony and set up quarters in the shadow of the barracks. I scrambled every morning to be on parade, leaving her tumbled on the bed, the place messed with food and dishes, clothes, the slow encroachment of dirt and disorder. When the baby came, it was a son. She was so warmed and glowing with her love for him, and mine for both of them, that it was as though a lamp was lighted in a place of shadows. That was before bitterness crept back into the room like cockroaches.

Six months after his birth, the army sent me north on a fresh tour of duty. There were cries of separation, promises meant and never kept and a swirl of dust from marching feet and the churning wheels of transport coming between me and the glimpse I had of her, the boy in her arms, waving. I sent my pay and letters, and messages for the boy, imagining him. I counted the days to my return on leave to play with him and teach him the half-remembered games and rhymes of my own boyhood. In my nighttime dreams he grew and strengthened, fathered as I never was. But in the stark daylight we put down skirmishes in the hill country, with more blood, more summary executions, crushing riots, breaking apart families and villages, leaving our trail of conquest written in the dust behind us. Then, six months later, the messages from her faded away, and one day mine returned to me, 'Not Known'. And so, I lost my son.

I sent messages, word of mouth, scribbled letters with each and every comrade posted there and to those I knew still stationed in the city garrison. But no response from her, only a vague rumour that she had fled north-west with the boy; and after the year passed, and I was sent to peacekeeping duties in Europe, I gave way to despair and hardened myself to soldiering and to the brief, intense distractions that come with the job. There are no excuses: I am only saying what was, what is, the reality. I was posted hundreds of miles away, and under a different sky, and in the hubbub of different voices and commands and duties, I lost him, and I lost her, forever.

But now I march again, through these foothills, towards the ring of mountains that surround the city. After forty years the memories I had dulled, suppressing into indifference, twist now at my heart, raw, snatching breath, as they did then. Oh, my son, my son, my feet tramp out as we swing steadily up the gradient, through the abandoned olive groves and the ransacked farms. As we halt for minutes to drink, to check the final orders, the stench reaches us. Burning, stale and pungent; the very odour of death and destruction. I have smelt before the stink of ruined villages and massacre, but not this. Not this desolation, not the ruin of a city. The marble facades that caught the sun and dazzled the eye are fragments that we crush underfoot as we move into unrecognisable streets and squares to relieve the garrison, consolidate the conquest. Gutted women, unburied. Children sprawled in angles, their lifeless limbs like the legs of grasshoppers. Birds that fly away slowly, insolently, from the bodies they scavenge. Flickering at the corner of my eye, other children flash like lizards in corners of walls and tottering doorways, too afraid to beg. Oh, my son, my son.

Later, that evening, my round of duties done, I climb alone above the valley where the city rubbish had burned – though all the city is rubbish now, and still smouldering and stinking – to the place where, all those years ago, I saw a man endure the unendurable and yet show kindness to a shamed and trembling young man, vomiting into a thorn thicket. His look has never left me, even in my desperation to forget the horror and stifle any humanity that might betray my weakness. I remember the tone of the voice of the officer of the guard: 'God, God!' he said, awed at the man's dignity. I was too young, too uncertain of myself to offer such respect: I could only flee and hide myself in her flesh.

And now, I stand here more alone than I have ever felt. Within weeks my service ends, and I take a pension and buy a small farm or a wine shop maybe, somewhere, for I have no roots. And as I turn, seeking a fresh wind from the hills to take the foetid stink of death from me, the half-crazed resolution grows in me, to search for my son, to find her if she still lives. To build again, to heal the wounds, to meet the sons and daughters of my son, and his grandchildren, for if he lived, after forty years, there will be family. There have been rumours too, mocked among soldiers, of the man who died on this grim hillside, and the followers who kept his name alive. That too, I can search out. Perhaps my son has taken my name, or perhaps she hid his birth. But her name I know: Tabitha, and it may be that she found refuge in a town or village north of here. That at least I might discover. And if all else fails, and there is no substance to these dreams, I will seek out one of these desolate children of the ruins and give him a home and livelihood. And so, begin again.

Reflection

Jesus wept over Jerusalem, foreseeing the consequences of the revolt against Rome: the utter destruction of the city and the scattering of its people, forty years after his crucifixion and resurrection. Perhaps he also wept for the dispersion of the Jewish people and their treatment at the hands of church and state for nearly two thousand years.

Here, in the story, is a man reflecting on his life. Events that have shamed him, griefs that are unresolved, the inevitable brutalities of a soldier's life in occupied countries. It feels very topical when we think of recent events in Afghanistan, for example.

But this man has had one brief unforgettable encounter with a dying man, and at the end of his military service he finds in it the hope of what we might call 'grace'.

- How do *you* think such a story might end?

I have deliberately chosen the name of the girl he was with, Tabitha, because I love to think of connections among the members of the Early Church. They had histories and struggles, like us, but we do not know their stories. But I have imagined a story here, and it is full of hope and healing.

Biblical references

Mark 14:16–39, Acts 9:36–42

SATURDAY

PIERCINGS

Teacher, Inspector, a restless class.
I had been advised. 'Go easy on him.
They're a difficult lot to manage
And she's quite capable of wrecking his plans altogether.
Loud. Can't wait to get out. He's doing his best
To pull them through the syllabus before the exam.
You'll spot her straightaway. And the rest.'

So I have sympathy as he struggles
To take them through the story of an ancient passion,
Sufferings and betrayal new as today,
Stumbling at horror,
Wondering at a daybreak two days after.

'So where' (he was sweating) 'd'you think
He went, what was he doing, those hours
After death and burial?'

The silence lasts for aeons.

His eyes flicker hopefully to the front,
The predictable triers.
The class stirs and shuffles, sighs.
Shrugs its corporate body.

Girl with piercings
Of lips and brow,

Black-nailed tips to fingers, hair spiked into thorns.
Jumper ragged over wrists to hide the slashes.
Her hand, raised. 'Sir.
Sir.'
I see his trapped eyes shift. The door, the window,
The front row. Nothing.
'Sir.'

'Yes, Della?' (O God, no, he begs.)
'That's easy, innit?' she says.
'He went to Hell to find his friend Judas.
He'd lost his friend. He went to find him.'

An indrawn breath.
Theology rocks.

Girl. Goth. Moth at the candle of self-harm,
Just so He will find you, even in its flame.

Reflection

The event behind this poem happened: the teacher, the inspector and the most unlikely student to answer the question – and the dazzling way in which she did so. I marvel at her insight into the mercy of God. Ancient traditions, based on a few verses in Peter's first letter, tell of the 'Harrowing of Hell' in those hours of rest between death and resurrection. In the Gospel accounts, we have so little information. The taking down from the cross and the burial on Friday evening. The women watch and *'go home and prepare spices and perfumes. But they rested on the Sabbath in obedience to the commandment'* (Lk 23:56). An unbearable time of waiting …

- What do *you* think was happening during that time of Sabbath rest?

- Do you think Judas found mercy?

Biblical references

I Peter 3:18–20, Luke 23:50–56

FATHOMS

The decompression of a sealed chamber.

> Stillness, and the hours fall like leaves,
> Limbs loosen from years of fathoming mortality.
> Cells stretch into huger life.

A day passes as a thousand years.

> Remembered,
> That first of all confinements,
> And the forced narrowing of birth.
> Love, joy, anguish, sorrow, apprehended
> Within the strangely heavy garb of flesh.
> All paths walked with seeming leaden feet.
> The eyes' ageless penetration
> Blinkered within the heavy helmet of the head.

> That first striding exhilaration of creation
> Until now forgotten:
> The pristine deeps of darkened caverns,
> Crystalline as light was spoken,
> The canyons of the seas, myriad with life,
> The vertiginous heights of mountain ranges,
> Forests of fervent growth.

Awaiting now the huge hilarity of resurrection,
Rising light and light to laughter,

Within unfettered elements
Of space and air.

Reflection

- Cocooned within the coolness of the tomb and the binding linen cloths, is there a time of rest and waiting?

I have tried to imagine what it might have been like, even for a moment, as the Lord of Life is so confined. Yet his whole earthly ministry has been a 'confinement', a narrowing and limiting of the boundless life and creativity that formed universes beyond our imagining. And yet willingly undertaken: *'Love'*, as Julian of Norwich says, *'was his meaning'* (*Revelations of Divine Love*).

Biblical reference

Luke 24:1–7

SUNDAY

RESURRECTION

The earth waits.
Hung among circling stars,
Lapis and silver.
Its canyon depths and mountain shoulders
Crinkled like tissue.
Fragile with distance.

Just as the full tide swells and trembles
Before the ebb compels
          its fall,
Or at the lowest margin of the shore
A fringe of delicate and powerless surf
Holds like an indrawn breath
Before the surge begins again.

Or the bare field,
Plough-ribbed, scoured by winter,
Releases luminous blades of green,
A velvet nap caught in a trick of light,
Long before the spring.

So, the earth waits.
Between tides,
Between seasons,
Between tomb and garden.

FOR THE JOY THAT AWAITED HIM

II

Therefore, this Man, this Prince of Life,
Is liberated from the rock-hewn cave of our mortality,
And raised to exaltation.
Therefore, his Name is given for all humanity:
A door set open to that glory
Exuberant in the heart of God before the world
Was dreamed of, before its speaking into form and being.
Therefore, his unimaginable beauty
Fills the limitless and radiant heavens,
Caresses the earth with promise.
At his return,
The gladness of our healed humanity's worship
Will join the angels' jubilation
In a restored and reconciled creation.

Reflection

Both of these poems risked exploring the implications of the Resurrection, the consequences of which we believe will, one day, reach beyond human beings to the earth itself and the whole cosmos. We wait, the *'earth waits'*, for *'a restored and reconciled creation'* … *'a healed humanity'*. And we are breathless with waiting. We face challenges to the planet that might seem to defy even the creative energies of God. We are in the middle of a pandemic that has shown us the marvellous courage and compassion of ordinary human beings and reminds us daily of the redemption unlocked by the cross and resurrection. Yet we also hear of the horror of suffering, and violence, perpetrated against the innocent. We live 'Between tides, Between seasons, Between tomb and garden'.

Jesus walked unflinchingly the road that he had chosen, knowing its cost. We find ourselves on a road that is not always of our choosing. It is often puzzling, sometimes full of light when faith seems easy, sometimes darkened and troubled. As we have journeyed through the events of Holy Week we have found Jesus sharing that human perplexity and struggle, always fully engaged, determined to accompany us. It gives us confidence to pray with urgency, whether we are holding in our minds our own distress or that of the ones we love, or the huge needs of our world, and knowing that we are heard. That prayer, most primal, most powerful and most transformative, with which our journey from Jericho to Jerusalem began, is ours as we walk the road that lies ahead:

Have mercy on us, Son of David. Amen

Biblical references

Luke 24:1–7, Revelation 21:1–5, 22:1–5

SOURCES AND ACKNOWLEDGEMENTS

A couple of these pieces were published previously in Wild Goose anthologies edited by Ruth Burgess, used by permission of Janet Killeen

'When the time had fully come' was included in the 2017 Lent Anthology *New Life* published by the Association of Christian Writers, used by permission of Janet Killeen

Stories first in *Recognition: Discover Yourself at the Heart of the Story*, 2019, Janet Killeen, Amazon Kindle, used by permission of Janet Killeen

Wild Goose Publications, the publishing house of the Iona Community established in the Celtic Christian tradition of Saint Columba, produces books, e-books, CDs and digital downloads on:

- holistic spirituality
- social justice
- political and peace issues
- healing
- innovative approaches to worship
- song in worship, including the work of the Wild Goose Resource Group
- material for meditation and reflection

For more information:

Wild Goose Publications
The Iona Community
Suite 9, Fairfield, 1048 Govan Road
Glasgow G51 4XS, Scotland

Tel. +44 (0)141 429 7281
e-mail: admin@ionabooks.com

or visit our website at
www.ionabooks.com
for details of all our products and online sales